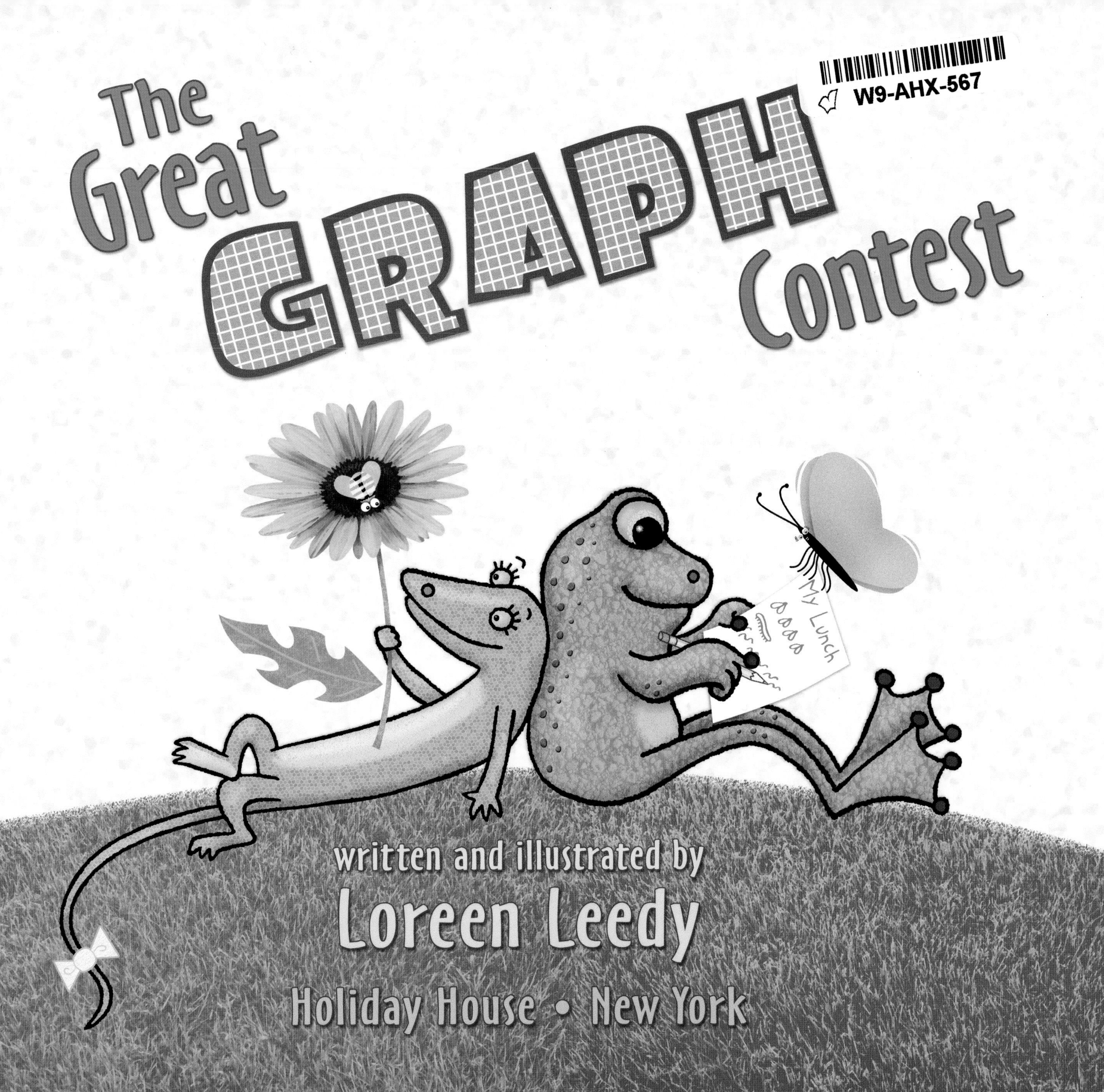
The Great GRAPH Contest
W9-AHX-567
My Lunch
written and illustrated by
Loreen Leedy
Holiday House • New York

Thanks to Martha H. Hopkins, Ph.D. and NBCT, of the College of Education at the University of Central Florida, for commenting on the text and sketches.

Copyright © 2005 by Loreen Leedy. All Rights Reserved.

Manufactured in China www.holidayhouse.com

3 5 7 9 10 8 6 4 2

Library of Congress Cataloging-in-Publication Data

Leedy, Loreen. The great graph contest /

written and illustrated by Loreen Leedy.– 1st ed. p. cm.

Summary: Gonk and Chester, two amphibian friends, hold a contest to see who can make better graphs.

ISBN 0-8234-1710-7

[1. Graphic methods–Fiction. 2. Amphibians–Fiction.] I. Title.

PZ7.L51524Gp 2004 [E]–dc22 2003062549

ISBN-13: 978-0-8234-1710-0 (hardcover) ISBN-10: 0-8234-1710-7 (hardcover)

ISBN-13: 978-0-8234-2029-2 (paperback) ISBN-10: 0-8234-2029-9 (paperback)

What is he doing?
Hello? Gonk?
Are you home?
Come in, Beezy!
You too, Chester.
GONK

Hi, Gonk!
What are you doing?
Hi, Beezy and Chester!
I'm making a graph.
THERE'S A FROG IN MY THROAT!
Do you like mud?
Zoomer Yes
Beezy No
Gilp No
Leep Yes
Hum No
Klick Yes
Chester No
Bugwort Yes
Yop Yes

I asked my friends,
"Do you like mud?"
I put their answers
under Yes or No.
More of us do
like mud!
Do my friends like mud?
Yes
No
This is a nice
graph, Gonk.
I have lots more
to show you!

Our Favorite Fruit Pies
Gilp
Beezy
Bugwort
Hum
Klick
Chester
Leep
Gonk
Cherry pie is the favorite? Yuck!
Where My Friends Live
Land
Water
Both
These are great! I like to make graphs too.
Oh, really? That's nice.
Of course, my graphs are the best.
Whose foot is the longest?
inches
2
1
0
Hum
Klick
Beezy
Gonk

They are not.
They are so.
WHOA!!!
Let's have a contest: You two will make some graphs, and I'll be the judge.
I'll give points for correct math, creativity, and neatness. May the best graphs win!
I'm going to win, Beezy!
No you're not, Gonk!
Oh boy.

There's a pile of rocks.
Hey, Gonk, can you make a rock graph?
That sounds really hard. Hee hee!
Only if you have rocks in your head.
I wonder if there are more smooth rocks or rough ones?
I'll put the smooth ones on one square and the rough ones on the other square.
Oh, I have to make labels too.

My graph shows that more of the rocks are smooth.
Not bad, but my graph will be even better.
Are more rocks smooth or rough?
Smooth
Rough
...thirteen, fourteen... there are fifteen smooth rocks.
I hope you didn't count me!
There are nine rough rocks.
I'll take a quick photo.

Look, it's a picnic.
Good, I'm hungry.
These cookies look yummy!
Why don't you make a graph about them, Beezy?
10

Let me think-
I see three kinds
of cookies.
I wonder if there
are more chocolate chip,
oatmeal, or sugar cookies?
I'll stack them up and
find out!
HEY!

Are there more chocolate chip, oatmeal, or sugar cookies?
My graph shows there are more chocolate chip cookies.
I think Chester likes it.
Only five oatmeal cookies are left.
That's because we've been eating them.
Sugar
Oatmeal

Whew!
Yikes, this juice is freezing!
Smile!
Chocolate Chip
Somebody's coming. Let's go!
Where to?
There!
SUITMART

SU
Does this bathing suit make me look fat?
SUITMART

ITMART

Can you make a graph about them?

I like these patterns!

MILLIPEDES

CENTIPEDES

SPIDERS

Over there.

Where are the suits with eight leg holes?

SALE

Do more suits have

flowers or bugs or both?
Both
Bugs
More of the suits have bugs.
Bugs are beautiful!
This is a good graph.... My next one has to be even better.
The suits with **bugs** are in the right circle. The suits with **both** are in the middle, where the circles overlap.
What if a suit doesn't have bugs **or** flowers?
Then it goes **outside** of both circles.

She looks mad.
Let's go!
Look!
The butterflies
are dancing!

They have such pretty colors.
What are you doing?
Excuse me! Could you hold still for a second, please?
I want to find out which color is the most common in this group of butterflies.

My graph shows that orange is the most common color for these butterflies.
And purple is the least common.
What color is most common?
This is too good. My next graph has to be even better.

Do you hear that noise?
It sounds like... cracking.
It's coming from Grandpa Zolly's house.
GRANDPA ZOLLY'S EGGSELLENT EGG-SITTING SERVICE $1 AN EGG/HOUR
What's wrong?
The eggs are hatching! ALL of them!
Hello, Mrs. Hummer? Come quickly, please!
I think Gonk is going to make a graph about these eggs.
?
21

Mama?
I'll draw a picture of each baby.
Hey, snakes and turtles are **reptiles**. The rest are **birds**. I wonder if more reptiles or birds hatched out?
Duck I
Snake III
Songbird II
Turtle IIII
Hummingbird III

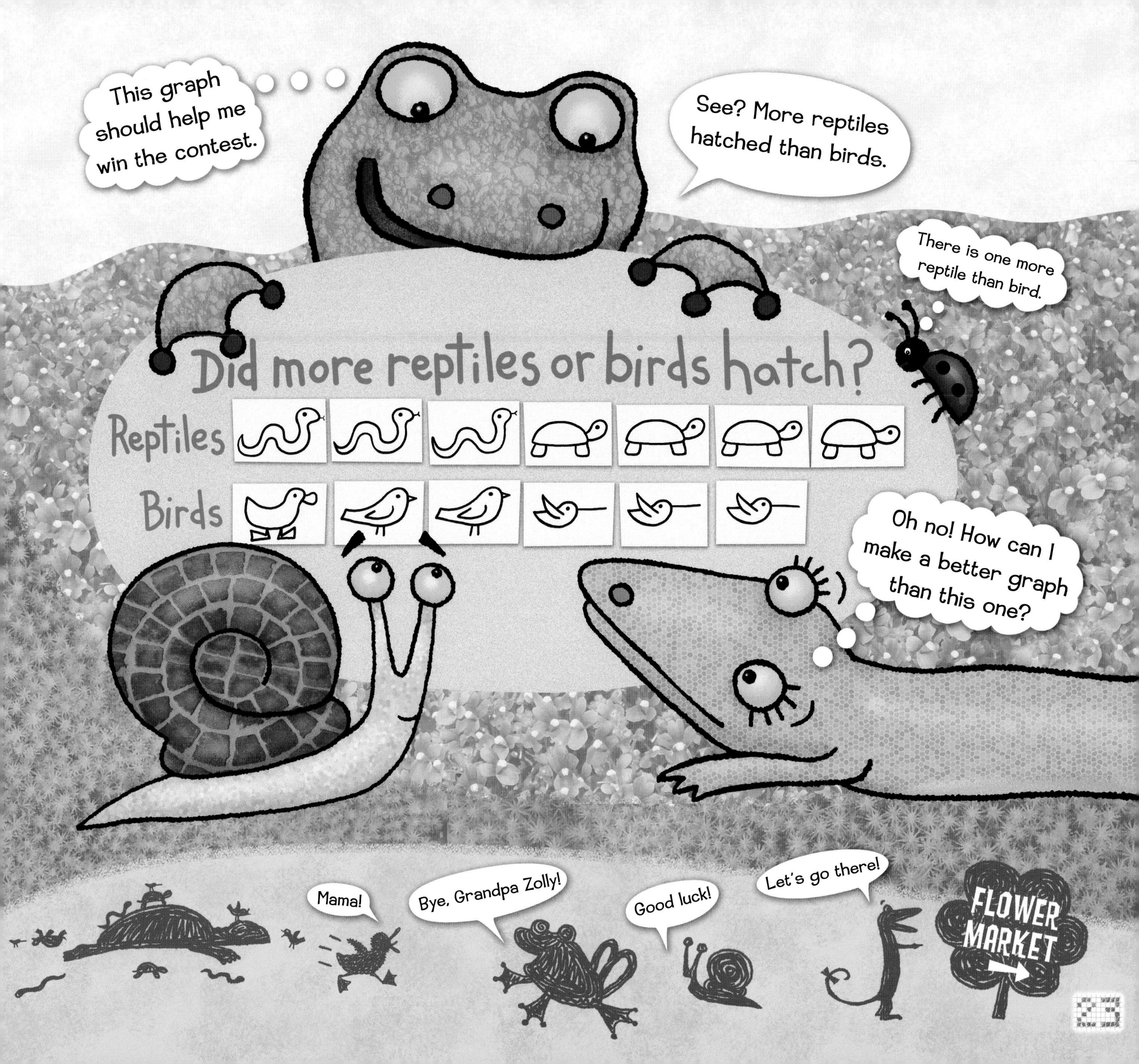
This graph should help me win the contest.
See? More reptiles hatched than birds.
There is one more reptile than bird.
Did more reptiles or birds hatch?
Reptiles
Birds
Oh no! How can I make a better graph than this one?
Mama!
Bye, Grandpa Zolly!
Good luck!
Let's go there!
FLOWER MARKET

Exotix Orchids
BUBBA'S BLOOMS
Flowers 4 You
I've got an idea for my next graph.
Excuse me. May I ask you a question?
What are you planning to do with your new flower?
I'm going to plant it in my garden.
Survey Question: what will you do with your new flower?
chipmunk:

Sir, what do you plan to do with this plant?
It's a birthday gift for my friend.
Survey Question: what will you do with your new flower? chipmunk: plant it slug:
What will you do with this flower?
I'll plant it in my yard.
Survey Question: what will you do with your new flower? chipmunk: plant it slug: give it away bunny:
So, what will you do with your new plant?
Eat it!

I took a survey at the flower market, and here are the results.
I hope most shoppers want to plant their new flower in the garden!
Survey Question: what will you do with your new flower?
chipmunk: plant it
slug: give it away
bunny: plant it
caterpillar: eat it
guinea pig: plant it
mole: give it away
woodchuck: plant it
squirrel: give it away
tortoise: eat it

What do shoppers plan to do with their new flower?
Number of shoppers
0
1
2
3
4
5
Plant it
Give it away
Eat it
Only two are going to EAT their plants?
That leaves more for me!
So, Chester, we've made a lot of graphs. Have you picked a winner yet?
PICK ME! PICK ME!
Whose graphs are the best?
PICK ME! PICK ME!
I should look at all the graphs again.
Oh no, that's another good graph.
Am I going to win this contest?

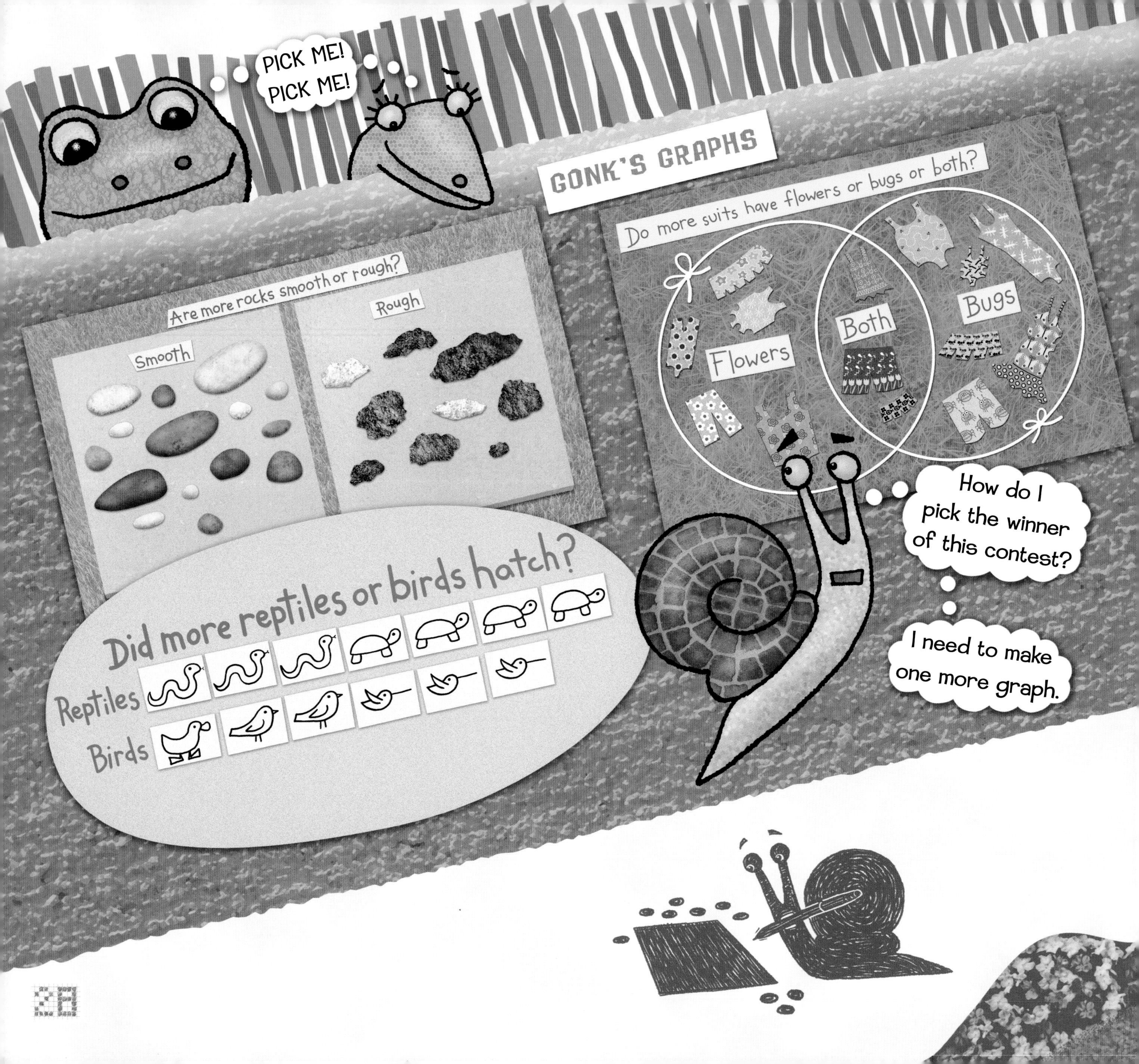

PICK ME!
PICK ME!
GONK'S GRAPHS
Are more rocks smooth or rough?
Smooth
Rough
Do more suits have flowers or bugs or both?
Flowers
Both
Bugs
Did more reptiles or birds hatch?
Reptiles
Birds
How do I pick the winner of this contest?
I need to make one more graph.

What do shoppers plan to do with their new flower?
Number of shoppers
0
1
2
3
4
5
Plant it
Give it away
Eat it
BEEZY'S GRAPHS
Are there more chocolate chip, oatmeal, or sugar cookies?
Sugar
Oatmeal
Chocolate Chip
What color is most common?
Congratulations!
Thanks!
As you can see from my graph, it's a tie!
SCORE SHEET
1=AVERAGE 2=GOOD 3=GREAT
GONK BEEZY
CORRECT MATH 3 3
CREATIVITY 3 3
NEATNESS 3 3
WHO WON THE GRAPH CONTEST?
GONK
BEEZY
POINTS 1 2 3 4 5 6 7 8 9

More About GRAPHS

Let's take a look at some of the graphs Gonk and Beezy made for the contest:

Pages 8–9: Gonk saw that some of the rocks were smooth and the rest were rough. To find out if there were more smooth or rough rocks, he grouped the smooth ones on one square and the rough on the other square. He made labels for the graph's title and for the two groups of rocks. It is easy to see that more of the rocks are smooth. But if a similar number of rocks were on each square, it would be hard to tell which group was larger; you would have to count all of the rocks. This quantity graph has two squares, but some have three, four, or more sections.

Pages 10–13: This bar graph is also made of real objects, cookies in this case. To see which kind of cookie was most common, Beezy piled up each type in a separate stack. If a stack is taller, that means there are more of those cookies. (The cookies must be about the same thickness for the results to be accurate.) The graph shows there are more chocolate chip cookies than the other two kinds.

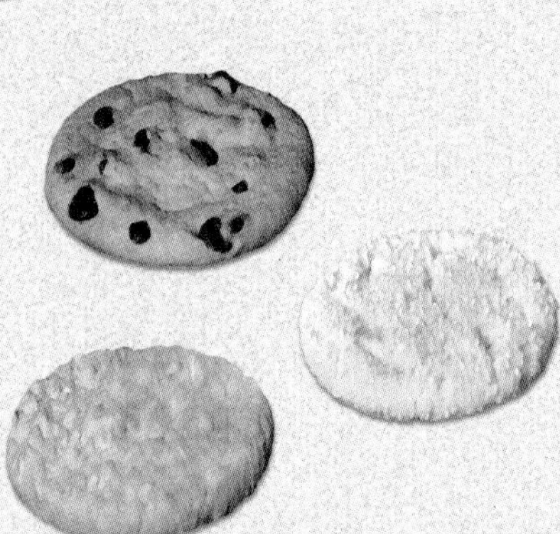

Pages 15–17: Venn diagrams show how things are alike and different. Gonk wanted to find out which pattern was the most popular on the bathing suits. He formed two big circles of string, making them overlap in the middle. He put the flowered suits in the left circle, the ones with a bug pattern in the right circle, and suits with both flowers and bugs in the overlap. As with all graphs, it is important to put labels on it so people understand what the graph is about.

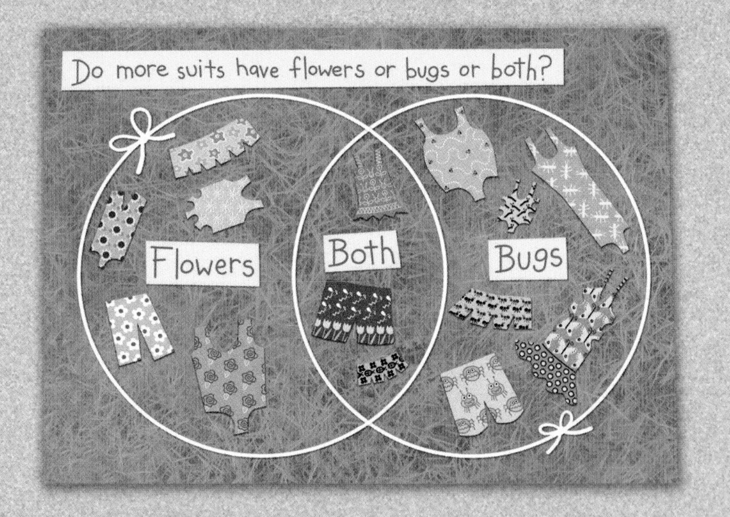

Pages 19-20: For this circle graph, Beezy cut a paper circle into twelve equal wedges (for each of the twelve butterflies). She drew a butterfly on each piece. Then she colored one wedge purple for the purple butterfly, two blue for the blue butterflies, and so on. She arranged the pieces back into a circle, putting the same colors next to one another. The graph shows that orange is the most common color in this group of butterflies.

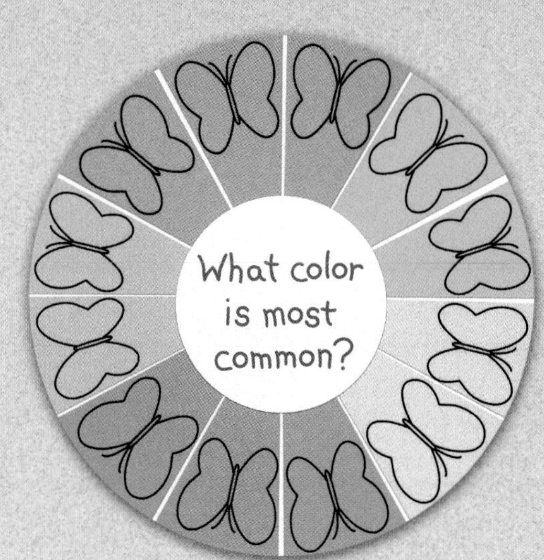

Duck I
Snake III
Songbird II
Turtle IIII
Hummingbird III

Pages 22-23: Gonk collected data about the kind of animal that was hatching out and how many of each. He cut out paper rectangles (all the same size) and drew a picture of each baby. He put the babies in one of two groups, either reptiles or birds. He lined up the pictures in two rows on poster board cut into an egg shape. The graph shows that more reptiles hatched than birds. This is a horizontal version of a bar graph.

Did more reptiles or birds hatch?
Reptiles
Birds

Survey Question: what will you do with your new flower?
chipmunk: plant it
slug: give it away
bunny: plant it
caterpillar: eat it
guinea pig: plant it
mole: give it away
woodchuck: plant it
squirrel: give it away
tortoise: eat it

Pages 24-27: Beezy took a survey to find out what shoppers planned to do with their new flowers. She wrote down their answers to keep track of the data. She made a tulip shape out of poster board and then wrote the title question on top. The vertical line has equally spaced numbers and the label "Number of shoppers." The horizontal line has the three answers the shoppers gave. To complete this bar graph, she made flower shapes (all the same size but in three colors) and for each answer put a color-coded flower in its correct column.

Make Your Own GRAPHS

Graphs are a great way to organize information, find out something, and display it visually. The graphs in this book are based on these types:

QUANTITY GRAPH
It may have two, three, or more equally sized sections.

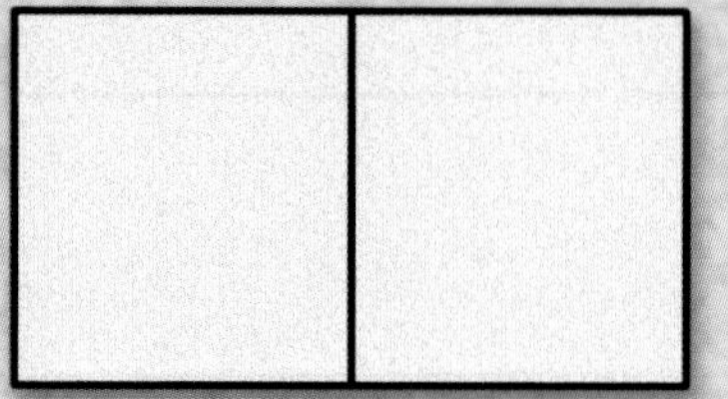

CIRCLE GRAPH
The sections may be equal, but they don't have to be. Also known as a pie chart.

VENN DIAGRAM
It has two or more overlapping circles (or other shapes).

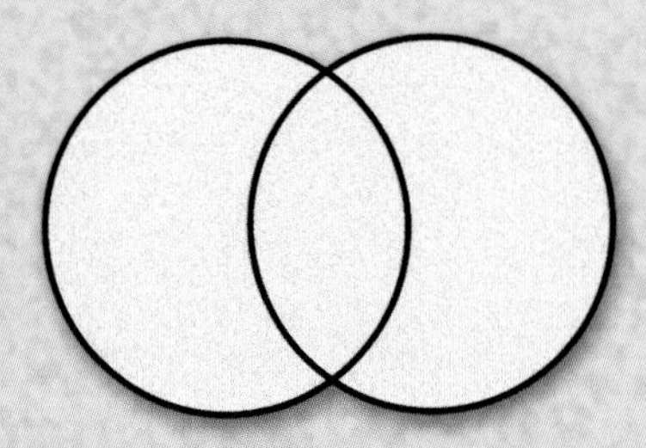

BAR GRAPH
The bars (which can be rows of pictures or symbols) can go horizontally or vertically.

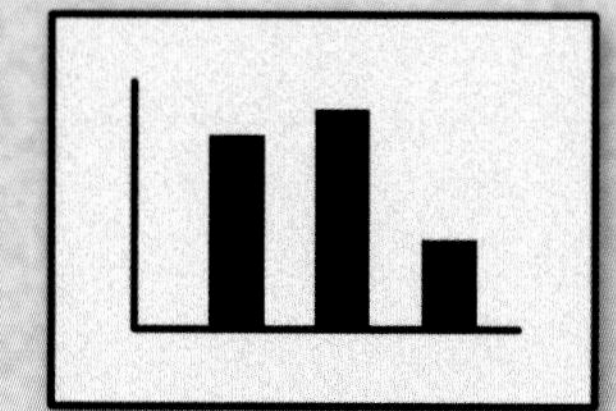

1 To make your own graph, think of a question to ask.

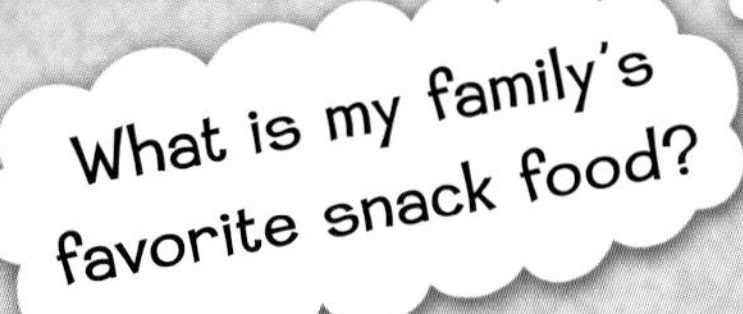
What is my family's favorite snack food?

2 Collect data and write it down.

Snack Data
Mom: dried worms
Dad: fried flies
Tunk: cricket legs
Me: fried flies

Snack Data
Mom: dried worms
Dad: fried flies
Tunk: cricket legs
Me: fried flies
Gran: cricket legs
Bink: fried flies

3 Use real objects and/or art supplies to create your graph.

My Family's Favorite Snack Food
fried flies
cricket legs
dried worms

4 Put a title and labels on your graph so people will know what it is about.

Your family likes fried flies the best!